IN
BEGINNING

Joe Johnson

SIMUL BOOKS
Portland, Ore

IN BEGINNING. Copyright © 2021 by Joseph John-Paul Johnson. All rights reserved. This book or any portion thereof may not be reproduced or used in any manner whatsoever without the express written permission of the author except for the use of brief quotations or passages for critical review.

Printed in the United States of America

First Printing, 2021

Cover illustration (*Expulsion from Paradise*) by dimapf
Back cover photo by Hanson Lu, Unsplash 2017
Section illustrations by Gustave Dore

ISBN 978-1-7365903-1-7

Simul Books
Portland, OR 97221

www.simulbooks.com
www.joejohnsonwrites.com

to Hope

and in honor of
Charles and Pam Scalise

CONTENTS

1. THE FIRST WORLD

ב	3
In Beginning	4
Endings	5
Caedmon's Hymn	6
Naming	7
The Lesser Light	8
Seventh Day	9
Tilling	10
The Poet	12
Fruit	13
Consummation	14
Consensus	16
Humanity	17
Hide and Seek	18
Euphemism	19
Breath	23
Inside	25
The Brother Sons	26
Babel	28
POV	30

2. ABRAHAM

Bill and Ted and Abram	35
Abram and Sarai Talk Theology	37
Sojourners	38
Mirroring	39
Oaks	40
The God Who Sees	41
Wagers	42
The Sin of Sodom	43
Grace	45
Fates Worse Than Salt	46
Then	47
The Daughters of Lot	48
Monolatry	50
The Longer I Live Away from Home	52
Coming Home	53
Becoming	55
Laughter and the Field	56
The Burying of Patriarchs	57

3. JACOB

Firstborns	63
How Blessings Become Curses	64
Bargains	65
Love Song (I)	71
Love Song (II)	72
The Daughters of Laban	73
How Jokes Work	74
Love Song for Leah	75
Reading Lolita, Reading Leah	76
Division	78
Jacob Loved, Rachel Loved	79
Spotted and Speckled	80
Of His First Eleven Sons, Jacob	81
The Burden of Being Most Loved	82

4. LEGACY

Siblings (after Dinah)	85
Benjamin	86
Indifference	87
Sin of Onan	88
Dreams	89
Namesakes	91
Bildungsroman	93
Wisdom	94
The Blessings	95
Love Limits Itself	98
Of Fathers	99
Father's Day	100
Of Family Trees	103
Ending	104
Acknowledgments	107

1. THE FIRST WORLD

ב

b'
be.
boom.

In Beginning

The beginning was about tidiness
and arrangement, forming coherence
from chaos, a sculptor and a universe
of loam, a painter with words for bristles.

The beginning was about joy. Pleasure,
perhaps. Mystery and hopefulness.
Delight in the designing. A poet
plotting out his great pastoral, having

the beginning, establishing mood.
The composer with a chord. Screenwriter
scripting a pilot with a cliffhanger,
a plan for six seasons and a movie.

Endings

The beginning carries an end,
like the seed that forms
its new self,
like the seed
that says,
This far
I will
grow,
only.

Caedmon's Hymn

translation from Anglo-Saxon, ca. 670

Now we should praise (Heaven-kingdom's Guard)
the Architect's might (and his mind-plans),
the work of the Glory-Father.
As he, for each of his wonders (Everlasting Lord),
established an origin.

First, he made (for children of men)
the heavens as a roof (the Divine Maker),
then the middle-yard (Humankind's Guardian).
Finally, he furnished (Everlasting Lord)
firm land for his flock (Almighty Lord).

Naming

Egypt alone needed a word for blue
in the time before grocery store orchids
stained the indigo of ballpoint pens.
A world without raspberry Slurpees
or Levi's stonewash denim.

The mystics and the prophets
forming the Koran, the Bible, the Vedas
never noticed a pigment as rare as Larimar,
never described anything as phlegmatic
as ER scrubs or the IBM logo.

Maybe the sky and sea of their day
were not so easily defined by hue.
Expanses larger then:
The sea-colored sea
the sky-colored sky.

The sublime scope,
the ineffable palette.
The sweeping strokes of an artist
who painted in horizons
who shaded with storms.

The light, he called Day.
The dark, he called Night.
The dry land, he called Earth.
The water, he called Seas
The expanse, he called Heaven.

The Lesser Light

The Giant Impact Hypothesis
theorized that the moon
was a fragment—
the debris, shrapnel, leftover scraps
of a once greater body
that did not flinch
in a cosmic game
of chicken.

Then Israeli scientists,
like my family with our home DNA kits,
discovered a contrary ancestry:
The moon was no more a descendant
of the hypothetical planet Theia
than were my siblings and I
heirs of Sitting Bull
and the Lakota Sioux.

Rather, the moon,
the lesser light that rules the night,
is an isotopic clone,
a genetic match,
the miscarried twin
of a beautiful daughter.

Half of a double.
A celestial precursor
to Abel and Cain,
to Isaac and Ishmael,
to Rachel and Leah,
to Perez and Zerah,
to Jacob and Esau, the unloved.

Seventh Day

It all resolves like a sentence
punctuated.

So soon
into the book of beginnings—

an ending, a seventh day,
a ceasing,

suggesting
that the story of creation

and creator is complete.
Whole. Final.

Full stop.
A resolution without conflict,

dénouement without climax.
He rests.

Then next:
a new writer lifts liberally

from yet unwritten plays—
a Romeo

a Juliet
a Prospero casting spells

in a garden where Iago lurks
in a tree

whose fruit
entice like a witch's prophecy.

Tilling

The earth,
in its own way,
lay wild and waste
without the worker,
the mini-maker,
the image-of
but no god himself,
the derivative

tending grounds,
shaping dirt,
forming,
organizing the clay
from which he came,

toiling
with hands
because he lacks
the words
or waft
to make from nothing,
to give life
with speech,

in constant contact
with his ingredients,
nurturer of the womb
that bore him,

reminded daily
that the difference
between sentience
and soil

is the breath
that passes
through,
the vitality
bestowed,
planted,
instilled
by a True Maker

as
every stroke
every dig
prune
rake
plow
quickens
the man's breathing,
spirit flowing
like irrigating
water,

the inhalation
and exhalation

the hurrying
and deepening

rushing
rising
falling
pant

of need.

The Poet

In his first words,
the man is a poet.
This, he says—a feminine
pronoun, an implication.

Bone of my bones, he says.
Or *bone of bones-of-me.*

Then, in parallel,
Flesh of my flesh, he says.
Or *flesh of flesh-of-me.*

This is his completed idea:
that what exists in this
other comes from what
already exists in him.

Then the *this*, the pronoun,
is given an antecedent:

woman, he reasons,
because she was drawn
from *man*.

Or *isha*
because she comes
from *ish*.

Fruit

Maybe it was Milton or Caedmon who
first claimed the Tree of Knowledge held apples,
which says more about English poets than
of the preference of divine arborists.
They proposed that any great fall must be

punctuated by a skin-piercing crunch—
a violent accent, percussive and wet.
Though I first read that story in Granger,
in the central Washington wasteland,
among the irrigation canals that

brought the river into the brush and fields,
where, for my first job, I gleaned high branches
from a shaky twelve-foot tripod ladder.
So, I imagine Eve succumbing to
a fruit that would, in the words of Donne's "Flea,"

"purple the nail": the mahogany-red
Chelan cherry, dangling amid fern-green
leaves, begging to be tickled or fondled
by a hungry finger tracing the trough,
the firm, subtle seam cleft like young buttocks.

Or God, the watchful orchardist—sure that
neither frost nor rain could ravage his fruit—
perching plastic owls, draping his trees
in nets, decorating the leaves and limbs
with tinsel to deter predacious birds.

Consummation

I lost my virginity in stages:
in the eyes, first,
then in the brandy-warm blood,
then in touch.

Not all at once
in some teen cliché:
a car backseat or a
parentless party.

But in subtle advances,
in the slow shift
from abrupt glances
to interlocking fingers.

Until I was twenty-two
on my apartment's
orange carpet,
and the gentle play,

safe in long-guarded
boundaries,
we went a little further,
took one step more,

and the moment—
a second, maybe two—
a thrust, maybe two—
when my eyes opened

and I withdrew and hid,
no longer sure
if I remained pure
or if it counted,

wondering if the start
was the thing,
whether Eve's loss came
in the touching,

the desiring,
the first bite,
or only after
she swallowed.

Consensus

The ambiguity of
"and the eyes of them both
were opened"
leaves me questioning

(1) whether Eve's eyes saw
and *then* she gave

or

(2) whether the fruit had effect
only when all humanity—
masculine/feminine—
partook,

such that unanimity,
not Eve's trespass alone,
made us wake.

Humanity
(Or, God Remembers Simpler Times)

"They were
funnier,"
said He,
"naked."

Hide and Seek

HaShem loses people,
even when there are so few.
The trees conceal Adam
from his view.

And then when Abel
cannot be found,
HaShem can't see
beneath the ground.

Euphemism

The scriptures use idioms
but apart from phrases
shaped by sheltering translators
they have little room
for euphemism.

Which suggests that when the text says
"and Adam knew Eve, his wife"
intercourse was incidental.

The first thing was the main thing
the truest thing: that
the man and the woman knew
one another.

Utter knowledge.
Love
Like
Empathy
Understanding.

Still,
as a man of my time,
I take "knew" as mere charm—
an antiquity
the polite code of prudish people
with limited tolerance for earthiness

shy and quaint in comparison
to our unflinching clinicality
our earnest and evolved authenticity
our sophistication and unfettered capacity
for being broad-minded

factual
blunt.

We tell it like it is.
No childish formalities.
No old-fashioned gentilities.

I almost believe this:
the eminence of the now over the then
the honesty of the stark over the poetic.

But in my morning run
three F-15 fighters
streaked above Portland.

The unapologetic roar
the monstrous potency
of audacious and righteous machines
that eschew subtlety.
They don't creep.
They don't sneak.

They arrive.
They overwhelm.
They overtake
their prey.

The first plane.
I imagined myself
as a Syrian
or a Persian
a Palestinian—
any soldier or civilian

of an alien country
that had something
we wanted.
Then a second.
I froze.
My tonic immobility.
My thanatosis.
My playing possum.

A third.
The flash of footage
from the night before—
a film on the '60s
on John Lennon
and Vietnam—
of bombs
more numerous than stars
falling
from open bay doors.

The planes
and their cargo
the great iron idols
of our complexity

progress that isolates us
from the chaos we create.

Aloof.

Pilots
2,000 feet overhead
—1,000 for parades

and shows of force—
at 400 miles per hour

miles passed so swiftly
as to be meaningless measures.
The gap.
The objectivity.
The anonymity
with which a uniformed
masked bomber
might
with different orders
drop its payload
accidentally
or intentionally
on a man
with children
and a cat

on an object
in an off-brand
track suit

on a being
nameless
and
unknown.

Breath

Ruach in Hebrew
pneuma in Greek
geist, I think, in Deutsch:
the ghost, the spirit,
the breath, the wind,
the animating force,
the exhalation of the
divine—

God, the bellows.
God, the source of life.

The breath in the nostrils
of sculpted dust,
the spirit that hovers
above the waters,
the oxygenating agent
in chemical reaction
with the animal,
the air of otherness
that blends with the flesh,
that infiltrates the appetites.

Without renewal,
over time,
the trapped air
that becomes
stifled and flat in
the vessel—like the
petroleum-rubber
staleness of an
inner-tube,

like the must
and dank of a cellar.

Such that the divine sets,
pun intended,
an expiration date,
noting of humanity
that dirt is always dirt,
animal is always animal,
"for he is
flesh."

The *ruach*,
the *pneuma*,
the *geist* of God
shall not remain
enclosed forever.

The tomb will be cracked,
the windows opened,
the balloon popped.

Inside

From inside
from the dark

creature stench
the slime
of creeping
things

Inside
with the
relentless
rocking

Inside
homesick
or seasick

Outside
towns
neighbors
neighborhoods

a world
to return to

dry ground
grass
figs
wine
coffee shops

From inside
the outside
still lives

The Brother Sons

3 brothers from 1 mother,
1 mother of the brothers,
3 wives of those brothers,
+ 1 father:
8 endured the water,
8 endured one another.

1 of the brothers
sees the mother
(the mother:
the 1 wife of the father:
the father
who is
blackout drunk
beside her)

This 1 brother
uncovered
the father's
nakedness
in the tent
of his mother.

This 1 brother
told the others
what he had
uncovered.

The 2 brothers
came and covered.
Then the father,
when he discovered,
knew the next brother,
1 born after the flood,
1 born after the others,

did not add up.

In sum
3 brothers from 1 father,
4 brothers from 1 mother:
1 father's decree:
the youngest of the 4
shall serve the other 3.

Babel

I.

The memory of flood
still lingering,
they build a tower, climbing
to the heavens
where God's waters
cannot reach.

II.

An angel blathers:
"It's as immense as
a mountain. Like one
of God's mountains."

The angel is drunk,
back from a decade
roaming the vineyards,
home from ground level,

from the worm's-eye view
where mountains are not
the only objects
as tall as mountains.

Like the Burj Dubai
or the Space Needle,
which I sometimes see
on a cloudless day

from the plane window,

if I squint.

III.

HaShem cannot see
from his office,
so he books a short flight
and descends to the city,

like an executive
called away on business,
like a tourist chasing
a new passport stamp.

POV

Pen in hand, I bloody the page
with comments on point of view.

Until now, I've trusted
the Tolkien-esque voice,
but here, in the episode on the city,
I'm distracted by the nonchalance,

by the scribe's ability to conspire
with humanity on the Plain of Shinar
("Let us make bricks /
Let us build ourselves a tower")
before switching
to allegiance above,
beside (or inside)
an anxious sovereign.

He (or she) travels freely
between thought and thought,
between Heaven and Earth.

And in this chapter
the narrator seems to contrive a crisis,
maybe trying to match the drama
and scale of the Flood
or the conflict of the Garden.
A sequel of sorts.

But I don't get the motivation.

Her (or his) creator, despite his capacity
to flood the world,
is threatened and nervous,
is insecure about how to parent.

This god confers—
with whom?
the narrator never says
(a different "us" than the "us"
at the tower's base?)—
to scatter and confuse,
to split unity
because it/he/she/they believes
that nothing people set themselves to do
will be impossible for them.

Which, to me, a parent,
seems a good thing.

But why fear them?
Why worry about characters
flat and faceless?
There's no antagonist among them.
No black hat or evil emperor.

And doesn't the creator know
that if he divides his creatures,
they will form clans
and conspire against one another?

Or maybe that's the plan.

(The narrator never tips
his [or her] hand).

Maybe the god character
wants dissent among tribes
rather than toward him.

But all this is speculation.
And perhaps I'm reviewing
an early draft.
Because when I flip the page,
the plot is scrapped,
and the story starts anew.

2. ABRAHAM

Bill and Ted and Abram

Perhaps the first world was as ordinary
as a trip to the dentist:
But Adam and Eve play like

characters in the *Silmarillion*,
flat and archaic, the stuff of lore.
Nor can I imagine Nimrod or Noah

at church or a Trader Joe's.
It's a little like that movie, *Bill
and Ted's Excellent Adventure*:

Socrates, Lincoln, Freud, and Saint Joan,
transported to San Dimas, California,
in an era of shopping malls and Van Halen.

Beethoven bewitched by drum machines
and arpeggiating synthesizers.
Napoleon conquering a bowling alley.

They are children.
Toddlers tasting sugar.

But then there is Billy the Kid,
solitary and ironic, a spirit-born
SoCal citizen. Gen-X before Gen-X.

Of whom, one of the teen slackers
says, "Billy, you are dealing
with the oddity of time travel

with the greatest of ease."
Mr. The Kid, unbound, flexible,
prepared for a new moment.

And so is Abram, after the flood,
after the Garden and talking serpents,
the original of a new age,

a character among plots,
timeless and of his time,
a fitting foil for his god.

Abram and Sarai Talk Theology

When I say the word
mother,
you think of your own.

I say *love,*
and you
laugh.

I say *god,*
and your eyes
squirm and shift.

Sojourners

Your offspring will sojourn.
They will wander and be enslaved.
And this—the aimlessness,
the homelessness,
the centuries of captivity—
will be a sign to you.

That you are mine,
that I love you.

That when you are underfoot,
when bondage has obliterated
even the memory of liberty,
when home is no more than
a madman's promise,
you will know I love you.

Not like the gods of other nations,
who spoil their worshippers
with land and food and empire,
with slaves and shelter,
with beds and bread and meat.

Those gods do not love as I do.

Behold,
I tell you a mystery.

Mirroring

It can go both ways:
The Hebrew can enslave
the Egyptian.

Sarai can own
Hagar's womb.
A little pharaoh,

decreeing the
death of the
firstborn.

Leaving Abram,
a little god,
far off and self-absolved.

Oaks

He left his home
by way of Shechem,
where a lone oak
marked the road
in a dry country
where all who
had been born
or planted there
would know it,
the only of its kind,
such that pilgrims
could be told,
Turn left at
the oak of Moreh
and never have to
ask, How will I
know I have
the right tree?

The God Who Sees

You are the god who sees,
the god who knows me,
even when I despise you,
even when you are recondite
and indifferent. When
we have nothing kind to
say to one another, we
walk on taciturn, until,
by accident or design,
we brush against the
other and remember.

Wagers

The uncle never mentions
his nephew
in the casual back-alley banter,
in the gamble.

The bargaining,
the polite but relentless appeal,
first for fifty, haggling,
then for forty-five.
The third petition.
No, if there are forty, I will not destroy.
Then a forth for thirty,
a fifth for twenty,
a sixth for ten.
For ten, I will not destroy.

The uncle pauses before
a seventh bid,
to raise or to call.

He quietly counts
his fingers, his toes.

The uncle considers his hand.
For five?

But for the lack of an ace,
he withdraws and folds.

The Sin of Sodom

The sin of Sodom,
according to my old congregation,
is sodomy—
an abhorrence
that defiles
an entire culture.

The sin of Sodom,
according to my new one,
is inhospitality—
a lack
of liberal
generosity.

But whatever
the sin was,
its stench rose to the heavens,
a charge against the Sodomites,
an outcry—
grievances and prayers
offered with such fervor
that God formed an envoy
to investigate.

And whatever
wickedness
deserved fire
and brimstone
was, ultimately,
unspoken—
sealed and encased,

quarantined beneath
sulfur and ash,
the melted silicone and salt
that formed
a glassy surface

magically
reflecting
only the sins
of the viewer's
enemies.

Grace

The Lord saved Lot
for Abraham's sake,
a sign of Noahic grace
or simple nepotism:

Like a judge who spares
her second cousin,
The cop's son who drives
off with a warning.

Fates Worse Than Salt

The way I remember the story told,
she was a warning about the foothold

of the subtle way culture seduces,
how our appeasement of sin reduces

our ability to know right from wrong,
how people give into this World and its songs,

its seductive lies, until, like Lot's wife,
we cannot help ourselves and lose our lives.

Like the story says, "She looked and was turned,"
an obvious moral in a choice of terms

that suggest complacency, decay
from freedom toward sin and shame.

But those phrases and the text disagree:
No, "She looked... and she became"—*came to be*,

Nothing passive. Two volitional acts,
two active verbs—not the verbs of falling back,

but the choosing to neither go nor stay,
the act and becoming of a third way—

like Daphne, who defies Eros and spurns
Apollo when given no place to turn,

who demands, "Let me be claimed by none
'Or change my form, whence all my sorrows come.'"

Then

Abraham
at sunrise
beheld the plain
in ash and ember
ebony and amber
in mist and smoke
and did not know
that any were saved.

The Daughters of Lot

Do you ever wonder *if*, she says.
    —Like if.
Like *if* we do nothing, then nothing will happen.
    —Like what.
Like nothing. Like nothing will happen.
    —But what if we wait.
If
    —Yes, if. What if we wait.
Then nothing will happen.
Nothing will happen if we wait.
    —Maybe nothing is better,
    I say,
    than the something
    you want to happen.
It will be easy, she says.
    —and I don't know which part
    she means:
    the beginning,
    the middle,
    the morning after.
It will be easy.
    —Then you go first, I say.
Of course.
    —Because you are the oldest.
Because I know that nothing will happen
if we do nothing.
    —And.
Because I am the oldest,
and there's an order for these things.

    —So she takes the wine
    and inside the cave
    in the moonlight
    she resembles mother
    more than I had ever noticed.
Tomorrow night is you, she says,
and she raises the cup,
and she says,
You look tired, father.

She says,
Drink.

Monolatry

If you ask the Egyptian, if you ask
Abram and his family, they will say
there are other gods. Gods who bring rain
and fertility, gods who give wealth
and grant victory. Gods with no opinion

on circumcision. But one of the gods
approaches one of the men, chooses his
worshipper, tells him where to walk.
This god opens and closes wombs, offers
land and shelter, sends disease and healing.

So the man agrees and follows this god,
and they have chats alone in the desert.
The god asks only for the man's foreskin,
which, as desert gods go, is not so much.
The god gives the man water and a home,

he gives flocks, he gives an heir in old age.
As desert gods go, it's a good exchange.
But this god, perhaps teased by the others,
asks his man for desert-size devotion.
He says, Take your son, your only son,

and sacrifice him on my mountain.
By now the man is in, he remembers
the wounds this god gave to Abimelech,
the diseases this god set on that house,
or the smoke still smoldering in Sodom.

Maybe the man's trust was not from fear.
But at some point, between grabbing the knife
and binding the boy, he must have questioned
whether, even as desert gods go, he
was chosen by one of the good ones.

The Longer I Live Away from Home

When tasked to find a wife for Isaac,
Abraham's servant asks,
What if the woman will not follow me here?

The longer I live away from home,
the more I understand Abraham's demand
that his son not return to left places.

Coming Home

I.

I am, this morning, in a bed
in my mother's basement.

I brought a woman I love here
to meet my people.

Last night, upstairs, we talked with mom,
my two sisters speaking most.

Maybe today, my dad in Moxee.
Later, I don't know when,

my brother in San Antonio,
my high school friends.

II.

Last night, when we drove over
the final hill, when we saw

the lights of the valley below,
this woman squeezed my hand,

turned as silent and opaque
as pearl, and, I,

knowing not to speak
pressed play on Coltrane,

A Love Supreme in place of words.
The Reservation hills in shadow.

III.

Inside city limits, Toppenish,
a lull between tracks, I pointed

to buildings, landmarks, to stories
from life before her.

Then we crossed the river
into Zillah, passing the house,

once my grandparents',
where, twenty-seven years ago,

I had, with a girl from college,
my first kiss.

And I said, eyes on the road,
"I have been here before."

Becoming
(Or, Advice to My Daughter)

Never marry someone
who is becoming.

Marry someone who is.
Unless you believe

the two of you
can become together.

But that rarely happens,
so you will probably

become alone.

So find someone
who can love you still

as you become
someone else.

Laughter and the Field

Laughter came by way of the well
from the south
and it was evening
and he sat in the field to meditate.

And he lifted his eyes
and behold
camels came
from far off
and Laughter walked toward them.

And from a camel
the Betrothed saw the man
and she dismounted
and asked her guide
Who walks the field
toward us?

And hearing his name
and being bound to Laughter
she veiled herself
as was the custom
in those days.

The Burying of Patriarchs

I.

When my grandfather—my dad's dad—died,
we held the funeral in the Brothers'
Cemetery, an Irish Catholic site

where many Johnsons are buried
and at least two more will be. More
men than women, all three sons divorced,

and none of us sure what will become
of my father's second wife, twenty years
his junior, when his time comes.

II.

Today, we stand for the patriarch,
who is now gathered to his people:
the two remaining Brothers Johnson

burying their father. The younger brother,
the middle son, my father, is here. He
organized, he ensured the twenty-one-

gun salute, tipped those needing tipping.
He begins, even as his older brother
and his youngest brother's former wife

(the youngest brother already in his plot)
have not arrived. And my mom is now gone.
She is with my youngest sister, who is

shaken and in hiding because my other
sister is here, with my mother's parents.
There was, in those days, a restraining

order, bad blood. And all of this—missing
daughters-in-law, missing granddaughters,
and a missing son—is the stuff of

patriarchs. The quiet conflicts
that manifest in murmurs, in side glances,
in shifting positions around a pit.

III.

When the oldest brother arrives, he is with
his youngest brother's former wife.
To another family, this would look noble:

the new patriarch, having brought Carol
and the last grandchildren to pay their respects.
But we know that Paul Jr. began comforting

his brother's wife long before his brother
had died, even as he was recovering.
They join us as the younger living brother,

my father, is mid-eulogy. And the funeral
continues—some head nods and new whispers,
but all remain polite, and family secrets

stay rumors as the Air Force detail
fires, then fires again. Then again.
And the funeral director taps

a button, which lowers my encased
grandfather into his reserved plot,
a few feet from his widow's future

resting place, as the unmoved matriarch
holds a folded flag and stares out
into a field of stones.

3. JACOB

Firstborns

I did not sell my birthright
as much as I abdicated it.

It happens sometimes—
the firstborn needs to find

his (or her) own birthright,
children are born out of order,

the patriarch (or matriarch)
comes from the middle.

How Blessings Become Curses

The father embeds his love for the older
in his blessing given to the younger:
> *Be sovereign and abound.*
> *Delight in the dew of heaven,*
> *the fatness of the earth.*
> *May others serve you, and*
> *may your brother bow before you.*

He reveals his disdain for the younger
in the blessing left over:
> *Live without water,*
> *reside in lands*
> *incapable of life.*
> *Serve your brother,*
> *and dwell in violence.*

Bargains

He did not leave.
He fled.

Somewhere between Beersheba and Haran,
he rests in the brush and sand,
among brown grasses
and coarse weeds,
unshielded from insects
or the sky,
with a stone for his pillow.

There, a dream comes.
A vision, perhaps.
A new way of seeing,
in which, for a moment
in the liminal state,
he sees the world
behind the world:

Where the night sky
is not a velvet blanket
pocked with pin-light stars,
not a barrier
or a cold unknown,
but a destination—

Where the night sky,
if the travelers
moving between it
and the earth
are any sign,
is the other side
of some migratory path.

A ladder,
a ziggurat
(the man's pillow its cornerstone),
on which angels ascend
and descend,
flightless,
coming or going,
he cannot
really know.

Invading or observing,
or only about their routine—
quiet commuters on a highway
wanting the weekend,
wishing they could stay home
and catch up on sleep.

But standing above them,
something
or someone
else.

And the man,
having heard light hisses
when lurking late night
on the floor
on his mother's side of the bed,
recognizes him.

The foreman,
for lack of a better word,
the ladder's supervisor,

or, if the ancestral stories were true,
the Creator
of Sky and Land.

And the god or whatever identifies
himself with a name
the man forgot or never knew
but that feels familiar,
a god who opens wombs,
who brings wealth,
who promises grand futures.

If the legends were true,
this god once commanded
grandfather to bind father
(which ruined all the family
holidays).

The god speaks his own name.
He says, "I am [----]."
He repeats promises
offered to prior
generations.
He drafts the man—
the refugee, the deceiver,
supplanter, liar, cheat—
to be his worshipper.

And this fleeing man
promptly bargains,
promising—
with the fervent and
spontaneous sincerity

of a drunk—
to give ten percent.

But not a tenth of what he has:
a tenth of whatever the god will give.

A rebate,
a dividend,
a tax,
a generosity veiled
in fine print,
an end-of-year cash-back
car sale,

not necessarily the best
tenth and
not necessarily by the first
of the month

but a kickback,
a from-this-day-forward promise,
an appeasement,
a token,
a coy way of saying,
"My faith is not free."

The man will not offer sons or lands
he does not yet have.

"Of whatever you give me,
I will keep nine tenths."

This is the refugee's vow.

This is conversion.
This is how he moves
from agnostic to believer,
recognizing that the family myth
had some basis in fact,
a god among the gods
here at this magic stone,
at this house of gods,
at this barren land
that now (or always?)
bridges worlds.

And the man wakes,
raises the pillow stone
into a pillar,
pours oil on it,
renames the site,
vows,
then continues on his way.

And with some distance,
like all dreams,
the dream of the god with a name
fades into a "did-that-really-happen,"
a delirium caused by stress,
a hallucination brought on by fear,
old campfire tales and family legends,
the natural effect of sleeping
on a rock.

And the vow,
the name,
and the worship

are forgotten

until the god,
recognizing the refugee
fleeing again,
descends his ladder
and battles

until the man begs
for a blessing
he already has.

Love Song (I)

Whether Rachel and Jacob
or Rachel and Ross,
we live with the promise
of TV shows and pop songs.

A glance, a word, a fluttery feeling,
a lifetime unfolding before us,
the weight of destiny and connection,
the mystical union of souls,
the warm and absolving reprieve
from doubt and loneliness.

Samantha and Jake Ryan,
his red Porsche compels her.
The explicitness of his overture,
the softness of her response.
Jacob loved Rachel, and Rachel,
lost in love, concedes.

Which is how a girl
in the romcom responds
in the major-key moment.

Which is how she,
acting her part,
behaves

before a boy
who claims love at first sight,
who mouths, "Yeah, you."

before a man
who tells her father,
"I must have her."

Love Song (II)

Jacob loved Rachel and labored
seven years for her,
then seven more.

Jacob loved Rachel, and it was,
I think, requited.
The two of them

equipped for something
their siblings seemed
unable to possess:

the sublime selfishness
of believing they should have
everything they want.

The Daughters of Laban

There is an order, Rachel says.
    —I know the order.
And this is what must happen.
    —I know the order.
And I don't like this anymore than you do.
    —Then why.
Because it's the only way
I can be given.
    —Then run away with him.
That's not how it works.
    —But.
There is an order, Rachel says.

How Jokes Work

It's like a joke: The Rule of Threes:
the first, then the second—just like it—
then the third, the pattern established
with one and two, the twist on three

usually a hyperbole, a non sequitur,
a play on expectations, like Johnny
Carson doing Carnac: Sis, Boom,
Baa: The sound of an exploding
sheep.

First, there's Abraham with
his hot sister, only she's really
his bride. Imagine Pharaoh's surprise.
Second, Abraham's son with his
version of the sister act. The
Philistine king about to hit some
of that until it turns out,
she's no sister, she's his wife.
Third, here comes the grandson,
a little bit of karma maybe,
meets the sexy sister,
says, I must have her,
and gets caught by the punchline.

Love Song for Leah

I buried it here in the middle
(in the uneventful and boring part
for those who read boring middles)

That I know the sheets Leah slept in
The kitchen she cleaned
The TV that chaperoned her bedroom

The malnutrition of infrequent touch
The confusion of eyeless smiles
The insecurity of comparison

I know the gnaw of indifference
The relentlessness of uncertainty
The humiliation of being the fallback lover

I know the erosion
The absence from family pictures
Standing behind the camera.

Reading Lolita, Reading Leah

I look for her beneath
the pages, trying to find
who she is

or what she wants,
like my grad school search
for Dolores Haze

concealed in the
narrative built by
her self-appointed

biographer. How he
hides her, how he
abducts her,

and shapes her,
changes her name,
concealing even

the etymology
of suffering, colonizing
her Spanish

with his Russian,
obscuring the girl in her
surname's foggy pun.

Here, like Dolores,
hides the unloved older sister,
the means to an end,

Leah, lost in her dolor—
serving the plot
of someone else's story.

Division

      Perhaps
    love can be divided,
  unless the parable is true,
that the servant cannot serve
two masters—that he will hold
to the one and despise the other.

Perhaps the heart can be split
ventricle by ventricle, beat
for one, beat for the other,
until the body finds a
new rhythm.

Perhaps the blood
may still flow,
though it runs
watery and
pink.

Jacob Loved, Rachel Loved

Jacob loved Rachel, meaning only
Jacob loved himself, Rachel being
Jacob in the form of the beautiful
younger sibling, herself capable of
practical deceit, whether feigning

innocence with her father's gods
wedged between her thighs, her
blood appeasing them (assuming
the menstrual claim was not its
own invention), or bartering,

temporarily trading her belovedness,
giving both husband and promise
to the sister in exchange for mandrakes,
a touch of Esau, though she may
have understood that Jacob was

her boomerang, her holding, who
could be cast or traded or tossed,
only to be claimed again when
it pleased her, such that Rachel,
prudent and resolved, wrestled God

into opening her womb, and when
given a son more valued than ten
sons produced by servants and sister,
she called the child *Joseph*, a name
meaning, "God, will give me more."

Spotted and Speckled

The spotted, the speckled,
the imperfect and dark,
the unsightly and unwanted.

Laban casts these away.

The broken and lame,
the poor and the refugees,
the second born.

These are the flock of God.

Of His First Eleven Sons, Jacob

Aside from Issachar,
all the sons are born
of a god's design,
a woman's scheme,
or a transaction
—and she conceived
—and he opened her womb.

As told,
Jacob is a drone,
a pollinating bee,
flying from flower to flower,
from queen to queen,
indiscriminate
in his own hive-building—

Not Adam knowing his wife.
Just Jacob a ram,
Rachel the ewe,
begetting a flock.
Israel the sire,
Leah the dam,
breeding by instinct.
The master the seed,
the slaves the soil,
filling a field with produce.

The Burden of Being Most Loved

Jacob lifts his eyes to Esau
and imagines what he would do,
roles reversed. So he, Jacob
meeting Jacob, sends his least-loved
women first, divides his children,
parades them in order of

dispensability, such that
Rachel and Joseph—the two whom
Jacob leaves for last—must hope for
retribution on the sisters
and the slaves to be swift, for
vengeance on the half-siblings

to be quick and absolute, for
the bloody but defining purge
that creates the quiet in which
they can walk or smile or touch
without glances or shame, without
the hiss of envious whispers.

4. LEGACY

Siblings (after Dinah)

"They despised how she diminished you,
how she made you smaller,"
Mom told me, after the divorce.

She said, "Your sisters love you.
And because they love you,
they wanted to beat her in the street."

"But," she said,
"because they love you,
they never did."

And I sat still, not sure what to say.
Because it is best to be diplomatic
when one can.

I knew I should have explained
that marriage is complicated,
that it is never fully one person's fault.

I sat there, waiting to be repulsed
by the sentiment of violence,
the anachronism of sibling wrath.

But, instead,
I said,
"I love them, too."

Benjamin

In the days before his birth,
as we had two years before
in the hospital room
with our daughter,
we listed our favorite names.

Rachel loved Joshua.

But I loved Benjamin,
a name that had always
been near, though
I had never known one.

And in the odd way
that the child knows his name,
if a parent listens,
our son refused to be Joshua,
could never be a Josh.

He was Benjamin,
Ben,
Jamin,
Ben-yə-mēn.
Son of my right hand,
My right-handed son
(as I joked to
my left-handed
father-in-law),

the brother of Joseph.

Indifference

So many winters later
the man who labored
fourteen years to be with her

which seemed to him nothing
for the love he had for her

buries the wife of his youth
without tear or grief
without song or lament

no record of sorrow
except a pillar to mark a pause
before walking onward

Sin of Onan

In our third year,
in my first marriage,
my wife and I
(a simple faith
showing its strain),
talked about it once.

She said she had never.
She said, It was a sin.
I said, Read it again:

That the story of Onan
was no more about self-pleasure
than was the story of Sodom
about sodomy.

Since then,
I've wondered
whether what loosened
in an act of close reading
was worth the freedom,

given the boundaries
and certainties
that afterward fell,
like Onan's seed,
to the ground.

Dreams
(Monday Morning before the Staff Call)

I can remember two dreams from boyhood,
though they were nothing like Joseph's.

                                              In one,
I'm eight, at night in my grandfather's garage,
walking between the Fiat 850—
as red as Snow White's apple—and the fridge
where Grandpa Johnson stocked candy bars.

Then somehow, in this small room, there's a
tyrannosaurus rex, who chases me
from the Snickers, who rushes me out
the white wooden door into the backyard,
where grandpa used to sit and smoke and drink
and feed the squirrels.

                          So I climb the tree
next to the plastic St. Francis statue
tending the bird bath and hang from a branch
until the beast goes away—or I wake.

The other dream is more like a recurring
character in a sitcom, the episode
never exactly the same, but this me
within each story—like Kramer in *Seinfeld*
tripping into Jerry's apartment—
always doing my bit: this me slipping
into the background, receding from
the main scene and, then, floating.

Not flying, exactly, because if I
try anything too high or too sudden,
I fall. If I draw attention to myself,
I fall. It's delicate levitation
that lets me lift but not blast off, rise
but not soar.

               Then, one day, the dreams stop.
Isn't that what happened with Joseph?
That he stopped dreaming and became
the interpreter of others' dreams?

I don't miss dreams until others share theirs.
I say, "I don't dream." Then when they think
I'm dodging them or hiding something
perverse and incestuous, I add,
"I mean, I don't remember my dreams."

Though, sometimes, even now in middle age,
I emerge from gray-haze nothingness—from
the unscratched itch of insomnia or
the timid workday nudge of my cellphone—
and feel, if only with the persistence
of a faint evening breeze or of ant feet
on arm hair, a light tingle in my heels
and arches, and I swear, if I can find
the right vibration or frequency,
if I can summon some buried knowledge
from the liminal state,

               I can hover,
I can ascend to the trees, away from
dinosaurs and the tediousness
of office chairs and dreamlessness.

Namesakes

I want to like Joseph.

We share a name.
He's the one guy
with good stories of being good:
fleeing temptation,
waiting patiently,
keeping himself pure,
staying outside the backbiting
and in-fighting of his brothers.

But he is either too good
or too innocent.
He seems incredulous,
almost overwhelming
with home-schooler naiveté,

like the eighth grader in the public library,
chatting with the librarians
who know him by name,
whom the boy sees as peers,
discussing Plato and poetry,
marveling over the secrets of colonial history
and how sad it is that other middle schoolers
can't fathom the pleasures of Bach.

For some reason,
and maybe it is evidence
that the world corrupts us all,
I read about Joseph
and how much better he is
than I am,

and I can understand
the thought process
that would lead men
to throw a boy
into a pit.

Bildungsroman

The rabbis debate whether Joseph
was arrogant, precocious, innocent,
or on the spectrum.

His nuanceless dreams,
his blunt confidence,
—to believe his brothers
would comply with his visions
—to believe the courts
would confirm his integrity.

"Remember me," he said,
from jail.

And then
he waited.

Wisdom

At last, he gained wisdom.

After being beaten, sold,
libeled, and imprisoned,
he traded innocence for guile.

Then he understood
that Pharaoh's dream
was a business opportunity.

So he shaved,
buried his prisoner robes,
and dressed for his moment.

The Blessings

Gather yourselves together, and hear,
ye sons of Jacob;
and hearken unto Israel your father.

For Reuben, the firstborn,
I have not forgotten
what you did in my bed,
and I leave you nothing
beyond what you found there.

For Simeon and Levi,
whose hands drip with blood,
whose hearts brew violence,
you have one another.

For Judah, Mr. Congeniality,
because the others could not fulfill their duties,
you get the crown
but not the prize.

For Zebulun, I bequeath the beach house.
For Issachar, I leave the fields.

For Dan, divider of my people,
you are a serpent tormenting horses.

For Gad, oh, child, it will get better,
but you will lose everything first.

For Asher, for Naphtali, the delicate boys,
lovers of words and sumptuous things,
hear the words I have for your brother,
feast on the blessing for Joseph:

Joseph, my dearest,
the rock star, the hero:

Dear one, you have shown
how right I was to favor you.
My amazing one,
my one true son—
your mother so much finer
than the mothers of your brothers.

To show how I adore you,
I will better the blessings
my father passed on to me—
That you are the only one that God,
The Mighty One of Jacob
(The Mighty God of Me),
favors fully.

Look at the kingdoms he has given you,
consider the servants and the flocks.

I bet on the right horse.
I planted in the right field.

Your siblings should thank me
for endorsing you
because you have saved us all,
because, God knows, if I had relied on them,
we would have all starved in the desert.

And, finally, for Benjamin,
who was my favorite
while Joseph was lost,
beware being insatiable,
be mindful of your pettiness.

Love Limits Itself

Each father allots love
like bread during famine.
Each mother guards charity
like a well in the desert.

A father must disperse shrewdly.
A mother must not squander affection.
You get Esau,
I take Jacob.

Surely, the love of God is not like this?
It must be overflowing—

Like the seas.
Like sand.

Love free to bless more than one son.
Love enough to adore even daughters.

Though Cain may disagree.
And Dinah has cause to question.

Sisters not remembered among brothers.
Sons clothed in mundane robes.

Of Fathers

Does God, as father,
father as God's men father,
seeing end from beginning,
knowing or prescribing
by naming the character
and fate of his people,
openly favoring some,
disavowing others,
dividing the feast into seats
of honor and dishonor,
opulence and crumbs,
adorning one,
leaving all else naked?

Father's Day

I'm in church.

I know no father among these fathers
who lives up to the minister's words.

My father never got there,
and I'm not much nearer.

This sacrificial, tender paternity
preached annually
mid-June, pulpit to pulpit,
by pastors who implicate
the failures in their flocks.

Lectures that begin with woes,
with Dickensian fables
of men on their death beds,
lamenting lives wasted on careers.
Dante-esque warnings
about hells of drug-bound children,
about hells of divorces.

Set against the unicorns,
the elusive and exceptional
compassionate warriors
who are able providers,
whom we flailing fathers
should aspire to be.

Missionaries and firefighters,
CEOs and accountants,
devout husbands bursting
with strength and compassion,

equally good at all things,
balanced between work and home,
lovers and servants and breadwinners,
unshakeable trunks of family trees
whose fruit abound
with doctors, pastors, and
professional athletes.

The anecdotes
and accusations
build to the hardest sermon to believe:
the straight-faced description
of a divine father
who lavishes goodness like debt.
God our father, the faithful father,
the father that all fathers fail to be.

Forgive me.
It's probably heresy
to say this divine dad may not be
so good a father as my own—
a father unable to fully give
what his children needed
but who gave what he had—
or even the father I am,
who, last month, drove four hours
and parked outside my son's middle school,
to bring him a fruit snack
and an orange juice
for his birthday.

Or maybe Father's Day
does God and fathers

(and children) no favors.
Instead, maybe the fathers I know,
the fathers I know among these fathers,
the father I am,
the father never preached

—uneven and inadequate,
a little lost, still figuring it out,
hobbled by wounds and wanting
more than he can ever have,
trying to do a little better
than his father did—

maybe these fathers
already know

what they are not.

Of Family Trees

The genealogies begin with the patriarchs,
the seed from which the tree grows.

But I begin with the leaves, first me,
tracing back through father, grandfathers,

stalled at the great crook in the branch
in Åyrd Parish in Blekinge, Sweden

with Alexander and his appetites,
with a name we have gradually pruned away.

Ending

It's a bit like Faulkner.
Maybe something like a marriage.

It's a little like *Star Wars*
or *The Godfather*,
the saga reaching its finale.

The ending had to come
the ending—
a little underwhelming,
more whimper than bang.

Like life.
Like the way beginnings hold so much promise,
but each choice takes away a little of that promise.
Each character, in choosing,
becomes a little more defined,
a little more damaged,
a little less of what we hoped they would be.

Which makes me want to go back
to the beginning,
to Luke beneath two suns,
to Michael home from the war,
to the Creator, content,
saying, It is good.
It is *very* good

And let it
linger.
Give it a moment.
Pause on the potential.
Imagine that none of this has to happen.

Relish the newborn smell
of a beginning.

Even though nothing,
once begotten,
remains
in the beginning.

Acknowledgments

"Fruit" first appeared in *The Purpled Nail*, April 2020.

www.ingramcontent.com/pod-product-compliance
Lightning Source LLC
Chambersburg PA
CBHW020010050426
42450CB00005B/400